darkness is where the stars are

patrick jones

Cinnamon Press
Independent Innovative International

Published by Cinnamon Press
Meirion House,
Glan yr afon,
Tanygrisiau,
Blaenau Ffestiniog,
Gwynedd,
LL41 3SU.
www.cinnamonpress.com

ISBN: 978-1-905614-50-9

British Library Cataloguing in Publication Data. A CIP record for
this book can be obtained from the British Library.

Designed and typeset in Palatino by Cinnamon Press. Cover
design by Mike Fortune-Wood from original artwork 'wall' by
jane jones used by kind permission.
printed by Y Lolfa, Talybont, Ceredigion
The publisher acknowledges the financial assistance of the
Welsh Books Council

Acknowledgements:

'bells of rhymney 2007' was commissioned by BBC RADIO WALES set to music by Mike Peters.

thanks to;
gary meredith, nathan sussex, stacey daley, chris durnall, hannah jenkins, jan fortune-wood, pete petrakis, trevor jones, richard dawkins, harold pinter, bob mole, les davies, lethargy, rachel trezise.

Contents

darkness is where the stars are is dedicated to:

irene jones, allen jones, jane jones, evan jones, ethan jones, elian jones, nicholas jones, james dean bradfield, michael kelligan, beverley humphreys, mike church, peter tatchell.

darkness is where the stars are

diary entry no. 4

stutter getting worse. stomach contracting. argument. silence.
children. dinner. silence. dishes. silence. noel edmonds's
houseparty. mr blobby. mr blob. door slam. rain in my face.
sit. under blacknight trees. i used to play here. as a child.
didn't think. i would end up here. like this. this. rain.
saturday night. see the tv screen flicker in unobatainable
homes. warm. life. noise. mine. cold. empty. detached. silent.
stare. stare. kettle. steam. stare. silence. sleep. slip. slip.
i said sorry again.

conflict tactics scale

shut the door
put out the light
dream of yesterday
keep everything out of sight

first the silence
the atrophic acts of attention seeking
then, the questions,
the foamfrothed mouth bile of control
then, the eyes
stonestare of schizophrenic electric

my home a cage
i cannot escape,
only endure
for the sake of my children
and their need for safety

scared to answer the phone
in case it is my family
so sit in stomach cramped stasis
as you isolate my identity
and feed it to your insecurity

because i am a nobody, a shit, a fake, a shadow, a mummy's boy,
a doll with a penis, a sexless mannequin. a father. a man?
yet i am everybody
who has ever felt
the nails in the cheek
the kick down the stairs
the stinging slap on shaved skin
the belittling tongue of torpid torture
that never sleeps
just waits at my side
for the wounds to bleed

then licks and licks until
i can no longer heal
and so, limp,
fat bloated belly, passive receptor of your hatred,
then crawl
crushed beetle
on all fours, to the door, an escape
but stop, and listen
hear my son's cry,
he's caught his finger in his bedroom door
i stand up, breathe,
blank out your noise
cradle his warm body,
close the door
put out the light
wait for tomorrow
keep everything out of sight
wish
we could be somewhere else…

the harming

you take pieces daily,
incoherent babble blisters naive eardrums,
not the slap, the hit, the rack of bones,

yet,

but the marching metre of maledicta,
the avalanche of atrophic adverbs
stemming sentences,

judgement delivered by javelin throated jury
serving loneliness,

silent mornings when only the children sing,
the kitchen windows mist with heat from your mouth,
halatosed hours drip from burnt meat,
plug sockets spark from human static,
catatonia sings like stuck flies
the living room

dies

under the strain of bloated bodies,
starving each other.

no flowers bloom in this drabness
no rings cling to quell this petrified present
saliva drools from varicose lips as you snarl your attrition,
and i i i am nowhere to be seen
i do not live here
i only exist,
head ached, congealed groin

treading water in septic tank
as the people come and go
even jehovah's witnesses get a smile,
friends sip tea, phone calls taken,
then,
the bipolared grin,
the narcissist's indifference
this
this is my existence
thoughts fester like the ready meals i consume to satisfy this hunger.

other than my children,
i have not touched another human, really touched, felt. held.
another,
for years, black out. forget. for death do us part.
a   part.
i roam the house, looking for signs of life;
a child's book, an empty cup, frozen photograph.

i collapse in bed,
the dormant stone,
the sleeping grave,
growing growing

push face into cool pillows
do not move
suck black molasses
staple lips to pages
swallow ibuprofen
remind myself
i am alive
i am alive;

for i am in you and you are in me and we are in us

for jane

she sucks pus from absent wedding ring finger,
holes gape like the separate bedded room we once shared,
while you, you sparkle starshine over our bodies,
entwined aphrodite dance,
the moonshine catches shimmering semen on your nectar breasts,
she measures the window for new curtains,
hooks, words i do not even understand—
vapid thoughts spill to halatose furtongue—
no happiness resides here,
she phones me at work, her stiff silence beckons my question:
what's wrong?
i smelled semen in the washing – have you been wanking?
she asks as if discussing shopping.
well if i was i'd come someplace more erotic than that i wish to reply,
instead,
i plead to please like an imprisoned bear,
afraid of the everlasting eggshells,
while you, my butterfly,
photograph your climax and hide them in my wallet,
and you, stone skimmed in summered light,
lay next to me in handfasted forevers,
as we dream, dream,
i climb your body, lick inner thigh,
suck labia through pink panties like a lesbian lover,
pour my suppressed lust into your porn star lips
while she, she, she spits in my face and scrams my cheek for not
changing our baby's nappy. happy? slapping?
and punches me from behind and her friend
pretends
nothing happened. nothing... ever... happened...
each morning, you smile when you wake and look at me,

porcelain cheeks and poppy lips speak love
in your demand for *hot sugary tea*
while she she she stirs stagnant pools of thought
to vitriol tongue torture, mustard breath
and
black hair protruding through white teeth—
i never wanted to wake up…
as your side of the bed beams beauty in books and ankle cuffs,
while her side, a demented coffin cackle of self absorbed ataxia afflicts
and the black milk of her dawn soaks the sheets in narcissia,
i bleed for you,
your eyes
your breasts
your volvic vulva of shelleyan verse,
your sleep spun hair upon neck, ambrosia,

next to me, next to me
she, invites heaving moustached female jehovah's witnesses into our
house to sit and pray and wish for paradise
on the other side,   the other side,
while you and i

find it,
here,
now,
in each other,
each other—

BLOCKED artery

i choke on the fat that drips
from the uncooked meat,
you prepare
fingers limp to touch,
breathless,
white ash, from windowless room,
swallow aspirin, break through walls,
take cover from your fury,
feel
the masking tape along ventricle,
fall away,

exposed,
vulnerable,

i ask for a bandage
you hand me a knife

i slash at my chest
cut out my heart,

red,

vital,

it   still   beats,

detached,

alone,

alive;

spring asylum

i fear you are going
to the place with many windows
that stare onto more windows
and share your meals with those you do not know

i fear your pyjamas will not be ironed
but reek of hospital
i taste the warm glass of water
that
watches over you while you sleep

i think of you tonight
yet lose your image in the mist
red lights mean you're leaving
white lights glare in my eyes
but darkness is apparent
as your presence here is missed,

may your mind find its step again
your eyes the tender glow
your hands the loved ones
that you left when you had to go

i fear that you are leaving
yet the walls can be doors
to those that know…

they

they;

twist your face
until it offends you

a disfigured appraisal
that fills their holes

the thoughts of suicide
that keep you alive
lead to
a much mauled mirror maze
of unsecured paths
that lead nowhere
but they,

under the gawp gaze of cloned masculinity
stay   stay   stay
as
indelible scars
make
invisible fists,

that still

fight the thin air

they,

left,

left

10 million christs

marching cadavers
inconsequential consequences
of another's lust and greed
stapled medals, a rosary for the cordoned
starving for successful failure

backpack messiahs
blinded by visions of paradise
unwashed feet caked in mud
a warrior psychosis
sold to souls
from
saladin's blood
on lionheart's sword
to bush's head
on bin laden's pole

crustacean crusade on overfed donkeys
a jism jihad on blurred video

an olive branch
an oxygen mask
a trident missile attack
purveyors of putrefaction
asinine dumb waiters
drunk on faith
fatah   hamas   hezbollah
idf   scientologist   taleban christianvoice

how many more christs
until we are all crucified?

moment of light

Certum est quia impossibile est
          it is certain because it is impossible
                                        Tertullian

the world turns
people stand still
stare from suburban windows
looking for a sign

the trees wait
eyeing the chainsaws
splinters and papyrus
guide our todays
as shopping malls and stainedglass windows
bring us to our knees

as subservience is all we feel

religion the new race
followers are easy to replace
so belong or be gone
as blindfolded women with stapledshut eyes
are paraded through villages
to lie beneath stones
and the love of men labelled evil
and rucksacks scream the word of god
place the veil, the hood, the orange boiler suit
to mark your ground and plead for enemies and infidels
and poppies flower in spilledblood sommed silence
as taleban lords harvest opium crops
to numb the masses
like bloodless crucifixion upon wooden crosses
and bush declares god is on our side
and blair expects significant...   losses

22

so.

today
i have become a born again

atheist
bow to a river bank not the parting of the sea
sing to a star not an invisible man in the sky
and

i pray for prayers to be abandoned
mosques deserted, synagogues closed, churches morphed into
poundshops
and the congregations will commune with one another
talk with one another laugh with one another

could this be how the shelling stops?
on a tiny piece of earth with no ownership manual
no ritual no prayerline 0800 number no tube of holy water
that guarantees eternal life
no jihad no them no us

then they shall all be fucking saved
from a lifetime of waiting
because
the verb is more important than the noun
hey
oh, mighty father?

cut-up/morning prayer

onward christian soldiers marching as to war
with the cross of jesus going on before
the confrontation that we are calling for
does not know socrates debates or platonic law
but it knows the dialogue of bullets the ideals of
assassination
bombing and glorious destruction
gates of hell can never
gainst the church prevail
we have christ's own promise
and that cannot fail.
there shall be no peaceful solution
only pen and gun
by word and bullet
by teeth and tongue
onward christian soldiers marching as to war
with the cross of jesus going on before
the sinners shall be known by their marks and shall be
seized by the forelock and the feet
run the straight race through god's good grace
lift up thine eyes and seek his face
life with its way before us lies
make a covenant o sister to make
their women widows
and their children orphans
to make them desire death
and slaughter them like lambs

and

let the nile and euphrates flow with their blood

we are brothers and comrades,

we stand side by side...
sidebyside
s i d e b y s i
d...

valley comprehensive

for ethan evan and elian

when questions become answers
when stars are merely facts
as the white board becomes all knowing lord
and red pens stamp our destiny upon our stooping backs

the beauty of learning dies
when minds cannot search and find
just swallow factations whole
when exam results and league tables
fire the engines of education
it's the premiership in the classroom
no room for the least able
the noose tightens on free thought
as sets slyly amputate aspiration

only those who will pass the tests
shall be allowed to take the tests

as
the unchosen
stammer in silence
tread water in clock watched anticipation
until their failure is legitimised
and school becomes brain asphyxiation

no wonder in the universe
no questions for their gods
i'd rather a tree taught me how to grow
than
tell a class how not to write

only those who will pass the tests
shall be allowed to take the tests

shouldn't education be
about teaching children

how,

not

what

to think?

man kind

for waris dirie

eyelids down
drenched in righteousness
spitting venom upon innocent skin

sworn
to secrecy
steeped in indignity
parading as
cultural identity

stapled sexuality
an egotist's litany
controlling lives
with rusted knives

stitched virginity
with thorns of masculinity

the mouth clings to memory
as blood in dirt
an indelible history
drowned in theocracy

even diamonds slip to insignificance
as the price of purity
rises as does
the perpetual misery

be it religion or cultural
that shape the fear of the clitoral
all are evil and genocidal

eyelids open
drenched in morality
spit reason
upon decrepit ritual

keys to your kingdom

for Reg Keys

privilege provides protection
from all the bombs and the hate
and affluence buys you abstention
from the battlefields of the occupied state

an accident of birth or
a victim of geography
the rules are not the same
for soldiers keys, tom and wales' prince harry

it is strange how harry's father and grandfather
parade like pariahs on poppy day
drenched in medals
splattered in ribbons like stapled cadavers

as,
tom's father, only wears one,
the face of his murdered son,
where no tomorrows grow, today
as the holes gape like a cenotaph sunday

so, pride is indifferent to suffering
and suffering must be for the chosen
or so we are told
or led to believe in educational history lessons
in a coalition of the willing
it is only those chosen, ripe for the killing

oh wilfred your words
stick in my throat
nearly 90 years ago you wrote
pro patria mori, the old lie
you warned us yet no one heard
and your words drifted like ash in the november sky
as now, today, still,
young men are sent to another trench
in another country
for another man's pride
to fight another man's war
but
only if you don't matter
to the country you're fighting for.

the naïvety

a response to gwyn thomas, national poet for wales

so, an old fashioned fairytale
directed by a few unimaginative teachers
now
proves the existence of god?

along with the tooth fairy, zeus, father christmas and
treebeard
which is fine…
in a story
not as some omnipotent being
some great cctv camera in the dying sky
or a reason to hate others in the name of…
we become one family… you say,
well, only if one believes what you believe
only then can we accept you
into our family…

funny, then,
how
joseph
had to accept his step son
into his own family,
welcome a stranger into his home
no questions asked
and change his nappies, feed his bones
and wipe his tears
as his real father
the first absent dad
lorded it upstairs
so think of this
next time you staple your sugarlipped ink to your
laurietised stationery:

your star is a rocket's glare
your wise men wage war on each other
each claiming their god *does not die*
and your stable is a million homeless shelters across
the world,
thank you for your poem,
it made me think, made me realise,
that i agree
god does not die

because he was never alive...

hymn

Any man who prays or prophesies with something on his head disgraces his head, but any woman who prays or prophesies with her head unveiled disgraces her head—it is one and the same thing as having her head shaved. For if a woman will not veil herself, then she should cut off her hair; but if it is disgraceful for a woman to have her hair cut off or to be shaved, she should wear a veil. For a man ought not to have his head veiled, since he is the image and reflection of God; but woman is the reflection of man. Indeed, man was not made from woman, but woman from man.

1 Corinthians 11: 4-9

cover my face
with burkha so unnatural
i'm so ugly in your eyes
or is it my vision is so clitoral

use my holes
to cleanse your souls
paint my image as your icon of immaculation
force the feminine into your crucifixion
an olive branch drowned in thalidomide
they said it would make the sickness go away.

away, away

For the pope and for the imam
all i preach is deicide
just like mary magdelene
i fucked jesus
just like mary magdelene
i have been deemed useless
i shall drift to dust
all around
within,

us
slit my wrist with rosary beads
blind my eyes with testosterone veil
turn the other cheek
as you leave your seed.

Go to bed with jihad so young
fasten my vulva with catholic tongue
decapitate me while i kneel
as all my sisters bow like culled seals

just like mary magdelene
i fucked jesus
just like mary magdelene
i am in each of us,

in absentia

i light a candle for the absents
the almost forgotten, the waiting, the worn,
a day light for the dark nights
a filament of throat from thought
i light a candle for the absents
the disappeared, the frightened,
the watching, the saturday fathers,
disneyland dads, happy meal patriachs,
contact controlled, access asked
permission prayed
the deadbeat, child support agents
no rights only deepest responsibility
i stare into the flame
see love and hate
unite
in
one
silent flicker
a black and white photograph in a golden frame

but

from the slit wrist
the rose will grow
from the distance
blazes the geography of the soul
like candles, we inhabit the night
absence is not abstention
what feeds the wick?
who starves the oxygen?

and

what man is not made from woman and man?

dandelion

for my mother and father

from the mouths of corpses
the seeds fly
into inside
the ocean is

weeds eclipsed by yellow suns
light stutters through
wait and watch
the epiphany said
collapse and start again
companion to isolation
friend of regret
slow breeze blow through time
a
child's breath mending sight
starting clocks of the unending daylight
so lay down in seed dawn
away from the deep cut night
inherent beauty of scattered souls
searching sacred earth for another place
as with these holes we become whole
fly fly away
what we have been is what we are
mother of millions fathers of forever
fly fly away
into the inside
as
what breaks, becomes
for
we are the traces

the traces
left for the next
the next;

white feather fallopian

*for private harry farr and the 305 other men murdered in the
First World War for so called 'cowardice'*

In the desert of your eyes
In the emptiness of your heart
Between the rock and the sky
In the gallows of your thought
As the thirst within your throat
Lives the white feather
Dies the peace together
Into the vortex of the void
Upon the insignia of your collar
Is the flower of the forever
By the flag of the destroyed

A crucifixion curse of commemoration
Choking in the fog of soul dementia
The rack of the tongue
On the neck of the young
Flies filling corpses
Bodies burnt fleshless
Anthems of betrayal *pro patria mori*
They're dead, can't speak, can they?

But from the dying
After the worms and in the air
An insolence indignant
An incitement resilience
From the wounds of knowledge
We find the knowledge of wounds,
An incendiary creation
From bullets, guns, shells and swords,

The white feather grows
From the mouths of graves
From the arteries of the dispossessed
Into the minds of the defenceless
Through the sand of the desert
To the mud of the trenches
The soliloquies of the somme
The verses of verdun
The elegies of iraq
And the prayers of paschendaele
The white feather speaks from the poppy fields
From the chiselled cenotaph concretia
Next to the waves of white crosses
The tired bookshelves
They will not die
They refuse to fly, fly away
They will not be hidden
A white feather fallopian
A new emblem
a silent anthem
In the darkest night
The whitest dawn
The bleeding truth
The ancient agony
From eyes myopian
In countries utopian
The versus, the hatred, the us,   the them
For, in the against
Colourless and borderless
A white feather fallopian.

the memory of steel

after the bombing of qana, july 2006

prejudice stalked you
gas crucifixes birthed numberless graves
shards of history stabbed solicitude senseless
you, prometheus, wandering shoeless in the desert
the world cried for you
stabbed oppression in your name
marched against your deniers
we hold you in our memory
still fight to halt it ever happening again

yet

now

you have become jupiter
as you stamp on weaker,
crucify those who are not like you
is this the final solution
to humanity's illness
are you the new ss, ss?

a suicide bomber, no dirtier than a missile attack
an israeli man no different to a palestinian child
a bullet is a bullet
no matter the cause
so
how can we clench our fists then close our eyes?
at this atrocity born from atrocities
a cataract crusade
just like before

you chant

shalom, shalom, shalom

and

the world closes its eyes
for a minute's silence
but still the air strikes sting with a vengeance
and your guns still roar
your guns still roar…
listen listen,
the traintracks freeze in despair
the barbed wire clings to polluted air
but your memory
is nowhere
is nowhere…

as now

the shoes are not on the other feet

the other

if i am the one
and you are the one
then
there can be no other,
can there?
as the eagle swoops
the blades blaze
the mountains weep
as humanity fades without a trace
what shall we do next?
will next do for us?

where is the other
the father, the mother,
the sister, the brother,
the other   of one and another
if i am the one and you are the one
then aren't we truly alone
instead
of all one?
if i believe in white
and you in black
what will we do when the rainbow comes?

what songs do we sing
what song shall be sung?
the other the other
we sing
for lovers, the others
in this end,
we shall begin

if there were no mirrors would we ever see ourselves
the other the other
everywhere but nowhere
the one in each other
the other in each one

where is the other
like a father a mother
my germanitas the brotherhood
all that we have all that we could
for i have heard the wounds of words
pouring from mouths
to echo
to reach

another
one and another
the other,
and
from this snapped vocal cord verse
i shall be unafraid
of the dialect of hate
the verbs of violence
and the full stops of silence

to find the other
in me
to hold the other
in you

lautre/otro/ander/altro/outro/alius/

alia

alia

alia;

incursion

i

a bomb is not a bomb until it lands in your living room,
again,
religion gets off its knees,
and attacks,
like sand thrown into eyes,
it blinds,
flags stab borders
and dialect drowns intellect
as the bomb bloated thin line
marks our space, our place
you and i
becomes us and them,
the birth pangs of a new middle east says condelozza rice
but the baby will never be born,
as children lay dazed in wrecked hospitals,
oh father, which art in heaven, we praise you
we have the right to self defence
but a warplane knows no morality
just another precisioned target on a silent road
in another country, another country...

ii

you fire
cowardly rockets
that sneer into small villages
then run and hide
pray to your god,
speak of your good deed
and yearn for a fake paradise

as retaliation cannot find you
only the family fleeing their home, unsheltered,
innocent victim
to a crucifix game
they did not begin...

dialogues with the deaf

for my grandfather and great grandfather

in the calm safety of my radiatored room
my freshly washed hand clicks at the white mouse,
tips of fingers tap tenderly at the letters
the quiet comforting hum of the computer screen
i dig into history
like the speed of memory
i find the site
commonwealth war graves commission
the years flash like teeth in front of me
i find the link to *the dead of world war 1*
like an afterthought
like an ebay helpline
i type in my mother's grandfather's name
two words that give flesh to this plastic
two words that have been
two words that lived and breathed,
loading, loading
my mobile rings, i ignore
i find the reference
then pay by code and credit card
for his medal card
then
it is delivered silently through an invisible universe
and my breathing jars, my hands sweaty
screaming like a star
shot like a spear through the years
the mustard gas tears
the mud soaked trenches, the hysterical yelping, the blood,
the bleeding, amputations, destruction, sludge drudge
and victorious speeches
a battered white and black photograph
of a medal record
two words,

this time amongst millions
two words of hope
and pride
i check the details…
yes, that's him
two words amongst history's narrative
i try to imagine his face, his eyes staring at the fields,
his fingertips blacked and gnarled, his boots, his tin mug,
his pencil letters, his waiting to return home
i read the card
theatre of war
france
applause, audience, entertainment… theatre?
then scribbled like a child's handwriting

Dead

all those years, filed away in some grey building
sleeping next to a million other *Dead* souls
unknown, unseen, unheard of
un

i save the photograph in my file
knowing i must never lose this document
turn off the computer
face the empty screen
face myself
turn away from history
face the future

prayerless palms

pressed to one and another
an other
press to soil
each in each other
useless hymns fade to dust
divisions fall between them and us
my hands must make the here and now become light
not subjugate altruism for a quick exit, an invisible paradise
the emancipation of desecration
in the name of earthly regeneration
prayerless palms
no footsteps in the sand
walk yourself,
no executed 16 year old girls,
face yourself,
no pulpit poison masquerading as passion
the crustacean crusade
the carnivore's circus
repent   repent   re p   e   n   ter
press your hand into mine
become
a peace detonator
let olive branches spurt from your hand grenades
use your hands to plant seeds,

to feed

prayerless palms

to lead

come,

there is   much   work to be   done.

sapflow

where drought drips
and doom looms,
like eyebright nectar
suck deep the fissure
of life lipping love
to where growth escapes.

sapflow,
against the grain
like evening rain
mindknow,
for earthshine
we must glow
sapflow,
starsoil
feed our roots
so we may use our once wings,
again
again,
sapflow,
spring sprung songs
of
going
of growing,
leaftaste on trembling tongue
branchburst birth
streamshimmer and mountainmarch
i know sapflow,
inkflow,
must go
to grow,

and fulfil those skywrote dreams,

that ground our feet.

rings of life

to the memory of 3,000 trees cut down by costain engineering under the order of caerphilly county borough council (plaid cymru led) to make way for the sirhowy enterprise way

Words are what reached me first

I read Whitman Hopkins Dickinson Thoreau Emerson
Thomas Frost Sandburg Heaney Neruda

They are speaking to us, linking,
They are singing

I see trees
green growing
        chlorophyll knowing
          mind inspiring
            soul skying
TREES
They are speaking to us

They are singing

Formless forms rising slowly
Unwatched— steadfast humility

A baby's cot
A grandfather clock
A writing desk
The children's book chest
This chair I sit upon
Onto this paper I write on

wait.stop.listen.
I hear the chains crack,
The machine's roar,
they are screaming at us
they are wailing
the snap,
the fall,
there shall be no going back
i shall make a wreath of elm, oak, ash, willow, sycamore
and place it in my mind
so
send us the coffins   the coffins

so when you next pass this space,
this road raging,
this urban clearing

stop.

wait.

listen.

think only this
there once stood
a woodland,   living

words— that leave me last

last,
        lasting.

~~treelunged~~

We   breath   what   the
Trees   purified
From air   soiled and putrid

The branches suck
And   the leaves   distil
The roots   feed
WhatMan'sgreedthrewawayand

STILL

Stand straight and to the sky
Monuments of dignity
Sanctifying you and i
While we breath safe air
Aswedriveandgloatandgleedandgashandmaimandcullandignore

As we pay back the honour and care

With the great human gift

DEATH

As we choke what helps us breathe

As we choke what helps us breathe.

flowers for the trees on mother's day

The trees we walked past
on the way to school,
now lay decapitated like terrorist victims

a field of fresh corpses
nature's first breath
man's everlasting curse

The trees you have spoken to in later years,
in thought in peace in yourself
gone to make way for a road to nowhere
now no one can listen to them.

The places you taught me to respect
have been cracked and attacked,
taken out like chess pieces
and
i am sad because you are sad
and
i cry because you cry
as the things you believe in
are torn and wrecked

i see you, a bird circling high above man's world
looking down upon the once forest
nowhere to rest
nothing to build a nest
no place to lay your eggs
so you fly fly away endlessly searching

but i know that there is a place
a rainravaged earthwarmed skyheld place
that lasts
it is in the wind, under the mountain, in our blood
it is all around us

a nameless nothingness that is here, there, everywhere,
it will not dull
it will not submit
it is the smell of sweetshops after school
it is in your handheld walks
it is the swifts in summer from your bedroom window
it is in whale watching coupon cutting sundaying sandwiches

it is learning to write
it is in the books that line our homes
it is in long division learnt from under the dining table
it is your flowers on mother's day
next to the photo of your mother
and
that, that shall not die
shall not be
evicted
cut down
deemed illegal
or have to wear white hats and yellow jackets
no
it is the spirit that surrounds
it is the acts that activate
and
the trees know that
the birds feel that
the skies watch
and
the flowers that you leant against your huge oak tree
one night,
dived into the earth
sank their chroma into the man corroded soil
dug deep deep down
and spread their seed
into a place that man cannot reach
and
i know out there

somewhere

in the wild wet wilderness

tonight

a birch a rowan an oak a sycamore an apple a hawthorn
an elm an alder an ash

tree

is beginning
and
trees   have   long   memories.

bells of rhymney 2007

commissioned by BBC RADIO WALES set to music by Mike Peters

Must we just sink into obscurity?
ASK the cracked bells of rhymney
Should we not yell proud like glyndwr?
CLANG the green bells of bangor
Yet we stood tall while they begged us to cower
SHOUT the silver bells of tower
Let's all sing with pete seeger
CHIME the rebel bells of tredegar
Let's not forget what we struggled for
CRY the blood red bells of newport
Do we lie down and play dead, dead, dead
CHANT the salty bells of holy-head
But we have the strength and vision still
ECHO the greying bells of rhyl

What can you tell me?
SING the fading bells of rhymney

Now is the time to show our unity
PLEAD the proud bells of treorchy
Let us make space to breathe, breathe, breathe
SAY the golden bells of pontypridd
Let's all vow to learn and renew
BLEED the blackened bells of fochriw
We won't fade into dumb obscurity
CHIME the glorious bells of rhymney

the sport of savages

asylum seeker in the forest
runs blind into thicket thorn
arteries pump fearfed blood through beautiful body
foreign
as locals beat the path to redemption
cuts his legs on hounds teeth bite
stumbles like a stunned boxer
though here,
there are no ropes to save
here,
it's the glaring eyes of xenophobia
the vocabulary of righteousness
the mouth of vengeance
disguised in the smile of savages
bathed in the oxymoronics of human rights and
countryside alliances
of culture and conservation
as the asylum seeker in the forest
falls to the ground
scared, scarred and shish kebab skewered
on a pissed night in oxfordshire
he takes to ground
clutching soil licking grass
as the spectators surround
and hiss and claw and point and jaw
as he digs and digs
away from the disappearing sky
as it all goes black
spews back memory of other tunnels, other places,

other hauntings
other huntings
as outside,
the baying masses take communion with their unnatural nature
glimpses of red   white   and blue
someone lets the dogs attack
everything bleeds red
the asylum seeker in the forest is dragged dazed and dying
out of its den
surrounded by freedom
the virus attacks,
bones wracked
as collapsed lungs sing,
its neck is broken
the blood river flows
as if returning home
away from here
away from here

the game over
the crowd disperse
work finished
carcass discarded
the prize
from new zealand prime rib
blood dripping
wine from france
and perhaps a little caviar
as the dogs clamped like guantanamo

the asylum seeker in the forest
is invisible
is silence
as inside the lodge
the talk is of victory,
keeping britain for the british
and the right of free speech
and assembly and the need to place terrorist suspects
under house arrest

a sport for savages
for queen and country
the language of damage
the moral right to liberty

no asylum given in this land
upon this earth
only the derelict dance of class and tradition
the right of the righteous
the epitome of moral contradiction
so next time you pass this clearing of red white and blue
remember
who assembled here, who sparked the terror, who hid the truth
remember
the asylum seeker in the forest   an unmarked   grave

the earth holds what the earth gave

mountains of man

in silencebirth we stoodstand
in frostfuel we starebare
in awe we wait
in what we failfall
wintering mountains of moltenman
in such this short sunlight
within such atrophic eyes
i see i am i will be;
windwashed rainslapped timeworn
eternities united in minutesmelting watching the
mountained sky
stay inside of me
but how this anxiety
how this temporality
brownburnt grass blanketing beauty
standing still still standing
like sanctity
breathing bright as childhood memory
this man
this mountain
this moment
must
last
mountains of man
man,
man of mountains;
in silencebirth something stirs
something exists,
to speak not is to vociferate
to ask the questions is to seek the answers
to hold still is going enough
within this burden of soulsomewhere stone
floods of sunwarned grass
through endlessened nights
tiny glitters of light lit

that
that shall never submit
like fractured points of oppression
we cling to this
a dissolute
epiphany
of
yearning

to;

to;

when we become mountains

for cancer research's blackwood relay for life teams

La esperanza muere ultimo
– hope dies last
Jessie de la Cruz

Stood like shoulders
carrying the plight,
if we become mountains
we shall find the light.
The rain carries streams
cutting through soil,
searching for release
stitching scars into soul.
As age makes maps of us all
organs falter, brain cells die,
yet the body will stand
still reaching to the sky.

So, the seasons come and go,
the colours drain
the grass dies then grows
but the mountain, the mountain remains
silent and beautiful
bearing the wounds of living
as nothing is perfection—
we all have cracks:

It's how the light breaks in

And,
As we walk through the mist
we know that this life, our living, is a risk
and the only way is to rage on, to resist.

And so,
if night should fall and the path lays hidden

we must remember,
we must remember
just like stars we need the darkness
so that we can glisten,
we can glisten,

when   we   become

mountains

meat

shall i live my life on my knees
shall i crawl to just survive
from the moment of conception
you label me a sinner
a fraud, a deception

my son, aged 5 tells me he loves everyone on this planet
a sinner? a failure?
strangled sunflowers seeking sun
drowned dandelions drifting down
even the trees tremble in tired gaze

we're all too scared of crucifixion
an olive branched verisimilitude
on my knees
facing mecca to make you feel better
torpid tongues speaking silence
your wine is not the blood
your bread not bones
they are mere physicalities

and we, we are meat
festering sores on junkbait skin
simmering salvation spitting within
the flesh the blood the bones the teeth
linking arms against impending death
sonic connections and passing thoughts
what makes us human is not your rules
but
the tiny step
the reaching hand
the scarred chest

as verbs are vulnerable
as i flounder, i drag, i fall, i live, i die
crushed beetles under nature's soles
i was god fearing penance pulled sin drowned
before i could say my 9 times table
in the child's silence of playing alone
to the dementia shrunk brain of old age
we make the tracks that shape the flow
no adam and eve in the garden
just breast and neck,
just stone axe and found flint arrowhead
only when you've seen the stars on frozen nights
sucked vitamins through dawn's shimmering sunlight
touched the bleeding bark in autumnal firethroat
watched penicillin course through sick veins
will you acknowledge our significant insignificance

i don't need morality from a historical story
the darkest habit is the inability to think
so suck upon the nipples of deceit,
they will never fail to provide
yet will always leave you hungry for more, and more
as the milk of righteousness drowns our reason
a vertigo of the heart in the face of another
so i am godless in the skies
and godless in my heart
i walk, without scaffold, naked unto the sun
i walk i limp i run i die, i die,
like the first three minutes of this universe
i am uncontrollable, desperate, god less
i am   earth   fire   water   air
no rocket's red glare, no mosque tannoy
just a stuttering soliloquy
a bulletproof symphony
i walk i limp i run i live i die,

how the emptiness filled

i used to stay awake
watching you sleep
that one night
excited as a kid on christmas eve
almost as if undeserving
almost on my knees
to some unseen matri-god
i would plan my days
around your school times,
even though i knew you would not come home
just to be close, if not there
lived my days in parallel
as you ran in the playground
i drove past, undetected
to catch a glimpse of you

tiptoed on glass splinters
always seemed to get things wrong
a tangled territory of terrified heart
that stalked the steps of the family home
as permanent places stung with temporary traces
home, house, up there down here, home?
the strangled dictionary of innocent tongue
an anxious articulation of delicate young
as paper is passed detailing times, days and dietary requirements,
controlling ink that chisels faces down
insecurity disguised as *best interests*
the washing bears the scars of separation
and the fridge yearns to be cleansed of chocolate and ice cream
i wanted to die for 5 days
leave a gap that went unnoticed

but shadows grew too tall
but in my trying
always a dream for what was right
as clocks fed my atrophy
daylight
choked my sight
i waited for the darkness
to drench

your rooms a shrine to absence
a still life portrait
of something so warm
they only came alive when the books were held
and the playstation light burned green

a claustrophobic carcass of care,
the days dragged as photos captured the time
in fading frame,

you grew, no parent can dam time,
new school shoes
and options evenings
i lost teeth
and a belief in god
just found a faith in myself
and an ability to stay
as now, your minds sparkle and shimmer,
you inhabit every space in the house, your home,
and your footprints mark your existence

i no longer stay awake to watch you sleep,
i no longer watch clocks or *get you back*
and for you, there is only one day,
and that is today, today…

black and white

the white feather, the only time the word the colour white
is used to denote negativity
failure, dispossession,
an incite to hatred
as here, now,
dissent is feared in the lands of the free
as blankness floods our minds
as today war is no longer declared
but continued
ashes caught in the wind
from far off places
we watch on tv,
it doesn't happen here. they live so differently. like savages.
it is all they know.
yet today.
another war
a notsofaroffwar
a not living room tv war
a here war
a now war
a white war
a clean war
a new war
an old war

your war

not my war
speaks my name.
but today,

i shall not salute
i shall not march
i will not build practice bridges in the desert
and my children will never wear your uniform
and bow to your orders
as your general holidays in the alps
no.
i shall wear my white feather with pride
i will throw away your prayerbooks
your bible
your koran
your torah
and i will wear your negation with beautiful positivity
because
cowardice is a gun
because
cowardice is a missile fired from hundreds of miles
because
cowardice is flying a plane into an innocent building
because cowardice is culling your own people
and because cowardice arises from fear i   i   i
am unafraid

i shall wear my white feather with pride.

shadowboxing

I place the suitcase upon the bed
as before,
i unzip,
as before,
i pack,
first the dettol stung cheeks
flu hot hidden holes, held in,
then,
the confusion, head spun days clinging to tomorrow
and my child's bedtime story,
a respite escape.
the hollow head of spent tears, torn, tired,
darkness milks the room,
i push the bibles deep within, fade,
as memory burns cracks in the ice,
i blink, knowing the unknown,
again again again,.
sediment of carcass devours coherence and i shiver,
cease to be,
feel then choke my now,
again, as before,
i find the christmas
you stole my innocence,
crushed fairy wings sleep within,
the unopened wine, sweep,
sweep the crumbs away, away,
drench yesterdays in nothing,
submit you screamed,
how could i when i had nothing to give up?
i find the gaps you spat at my mother,
patch it with love, love.

dead days and insomnia slow nights,
hold. hold still, focus, one, be there, gone,
be there,
there, shaking recollected in safety,
slow, inhale, heal, here, hear?

your perfume your halatosed tongue,
your jewels the thorns of briar bush,
your make-up my blood on your lip,
bury, bury,   bury,
in the suitcase cave,
the comforting grave,
so close the door,
open the curtains,
feel the sunlight upon my face,

zipped,
packed,

but not as before,

of you,

no   trace;

the love of blood

From space, there are no borders – Russian astronaut

will
fail
will eventually bleed
fed by ignorance
will die like soldiers upon somme battlefields
will be nothing
if blood is our god
to belong is not to bleed
but congeal like putrid jelly
in the failing of flowing
is the avoidance of knowing
so you cling to your family tree
not that soul that is nothing
and how your blood is nothing
nothing
but a biological necessity
love your blood and you shall bleed
the blood of hatred fear oppression
blood out of fear out of pain concealed—
but the blood of love shall outlast your love of blood
for belonging is not an artery flow
the blood of love flows knows is will
is healing sealing full of feeling
never judging desecrating
and the blood of love shall rise overflow
and know
that belonging is not where you come from but what you are
shall rise
drowning
the love of blood
until
it bleeds
into
knowledge not judgement—

sectaria

i believe you believe what i believe is
wrong,
so you believe that i believe what you believe is wrong is right,
wrong,
i believe what i believe is right
you believe in wrong

i believe in something i can't see
but is,
you believe in something you can't see
but is not,
we believe in something we both can't see
but...
i blow you up because you can't see
the same thing i can't see but
know that exists,
that makes me good and you evil,

i blow myself up because i will be saved and be with the one
i cannot see and in doing so
you will be one less and cease to exist,
you blow me up because you will be saved and be with the one
you cannot see and in doing so
i will be one less and cease to exist but you are wrong
because i believe not to believe is wrong
and i shall carry on until there are no unbelievers left
right?

darkness is where the stars are

1. solitas

i once lived life with my hands covering my head
afraid to look up, scared of what it would bring,
swallowed grey skies,
grew bloated on emptiness that consumed,
dying, dying, i lived for her, lived to appease her moods,
trod perpetual eggshell floor,
cowered from myself,
coward to herselfserving eyes,
wake to doom. steamed cars starving at night
bowed to her altar,
i, an alienated abscess of ache,
identity splintered. groin congealed. neckcracked.
afraid to move in bed. petrified to get up. and out.
fear fed and fallow fucks
i went to the mountain i cried in the cemetery,
i sensed solitude made friends with death
stem cell sympathy void of vision
i watched other couples, jealous of their normality
walked on invisible enmity,
dreamt of old age aloneness of passivity,
i lived with my hands sheltering my head
a threat of violence born from insecurity
dripfed days and hands holding nothing
constantly stuck in silence,
stuck, stuttered, sunk like stones under water

i held my breath,

i hid a seed beneath the concrete
i planted a sun under the stairs
i inked a poem to the stars
stitched words into secret places

2. *stimmung*

I don't believe it. Listen, it is quiet, calm. I can feel the sunlight on my face and not feel guilty anymore, I can hear the trains go through the tunnel and not feel I want to jump in front of one, anymore.
I can feel the rise and fall of my breathing and not want to choke from the snap of the rope upon my neck, anymore. I look around our home. Feel the bookshelves whisper answers. Touch the photos that paint our lives. Sense the stillness that bursts with life.

The house is so quiet; my sons are peacefully sleeping next door... my handfasted lover, here, next to me. They used to only be allowed to stay over for one night every two weeks – one night? You can't be a father in one night...
But now, they stay here whenever they want to and, that's normal, and kids like normality, they can put the posters they like on their wall and we can watch the football, go on holidays, laugh.

Plan tomorrow, yeah, see tomorrow we're going to walk right to the top of the mountain, you can see for miles there, I hope it's a nice day... I think it will be... tomorrow... We sleep. We wake. We have breakfast. We wash. We dress. We tidy the house. We make sandwiches and a flask... We walk the mountain, tomorrow, yes tomorrow.

See, when someone hits you, pushes you down the stairs, tells you you are nothing, isolates you from your family, makes day to day life unbearable, you, you start to believe in some glorious afterlife, a place of flowers not fists, of peace not hate... and you almost give up living... but I know there is no such place... that's what abuse does to you, makes you lose faith that there is order and continuity in life.

So you start to believe in some fucking invisible entity where you'll be cared for unconditionally, but that's what the abuser wants you to do so they can continue doing what they do best... destroying every part of you...

But that was yesterday and on that day when I finally said no, no, no more— I closed the door, her door and I walked to the sunlight and it was my sunlight and I exhaled for the first time in years, and today, for the first time, I know there is a tomorrow. I bow to godless altar of unified skin and skynourished bodies. The wind severs branches to launch seeds to new soil, then so have I, been broken to grow fresh life, somewhere else. My hands by my side. There is love. There is order. There is continuity... there is me... and there is you...   .

notes:

'moment of light' – the quote from Tertullian (a second – third century theologian) – *Certum est quia impossibile est* (it is certain because it is impossible) is from *De Carne Christi* (5.4).

'cut-up/morning prayer' is a found poem using Al Qaeda handbook statements and the Christian Hymns 'Onward Christian Soldiers', words by Sabine Baring-Gould, 1871, and 'Fight the good fight', words by John Monsell, 1863.

'man kind' – Waris Dirie is a former model and humanitarian worker from Somalia, who had her genitals hacked away and vagina sewn up at the age of five.

The quote in 'keys to the kingdom' is from Wilfred Owen's 'Dulce et Decorum est', written in 1917 and posthumously published in 1920.

'hymn' – The lines from 1 Corinthians 11: 4-9 are quoted from New Revised Standard Version Bible, copyright 1989, Division of Christian Education of the National Council of the Churches of Christ in the United States of America. Used by permission. All rights reserved.

'when we become mountains' – 'hope dies last' was a phrase used by Jessie de la Cruz, a farm worker who was amongst the first women to assist Cesar Chavez in organizing the Farm Workers Union in the US.

'darkness is where the stars are' – 'stimmung' is German for 'mood' and is generally applied to 'tuning'. It is used here to denote the ethos and sense of intimacy that is created by a room.